MW00675765
The fruit
of the Spirit
is love, joy,
peace,
patience,
kindness,
goodness,
faithfulness,
gentleness
and
self-control.
Galatians 5:22-23

SESSION ONE

GROW
LOVE

Coleslaw, anyone?

This 7-foot cabbage won third prize at the Alaska State Fair.

Sometimes after a cold night, giant cabbages warming in the sun actually explode—shredded cabbage flies everywhere!

Wacky World Records

Geneva Emmons of Washington State, grew a 1,262-pound pumpkin.

Some people in England grew a tomato plant 65 feet tall!

Farm Grown

Circle everything you see that grows.

Jesus' Life Shows Love

Matthew 4:23-25; 26:3-4; Luke 2:4-7,52; 23:33-34; 24

1 God sent Jesus to be born on Earth.
Draw baby Jesus in the manger.

3 Jesus talked to people about God.
Draw people listening to Jesus.

2 Jesus made sick people well.

4 Jesus died.
But now He is alive.
He forgives and loves us.

BIG, BIG Love

Draw a way you can show love at the place named on each fruit.

at scho

at home

BIBLE MEMORY VERSE

"[Jesus said,] 'My command is th

in your neighborhood

ve each other as I have loved you.'" John 15:12

In North Dakota, Dean West won two ribbons for his sheep, Eva. YIPPEE!

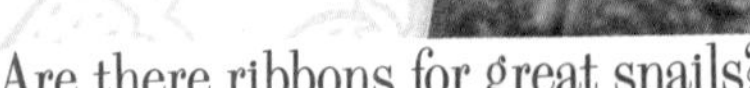

Are there ribbons for great snails?

Farmyard Funnies
with
CHICK 'N SCRATCH

HEY, SCRATCH, WHAT DO YOU CALL STRAWBERRIES WHEN THEY'RE SAD?

I DON'T KNOW, CHICK. WHAT?

BLUEBERRIES!
!

HIDDEN MESSAGE

- **Use the Color Key below to color the spaces.**
- **Look through a piece of red cellophane.**

What do you see?

Color Key

R = Red O = Orange Y = Yellow
G = Green B = Blue P = Purple

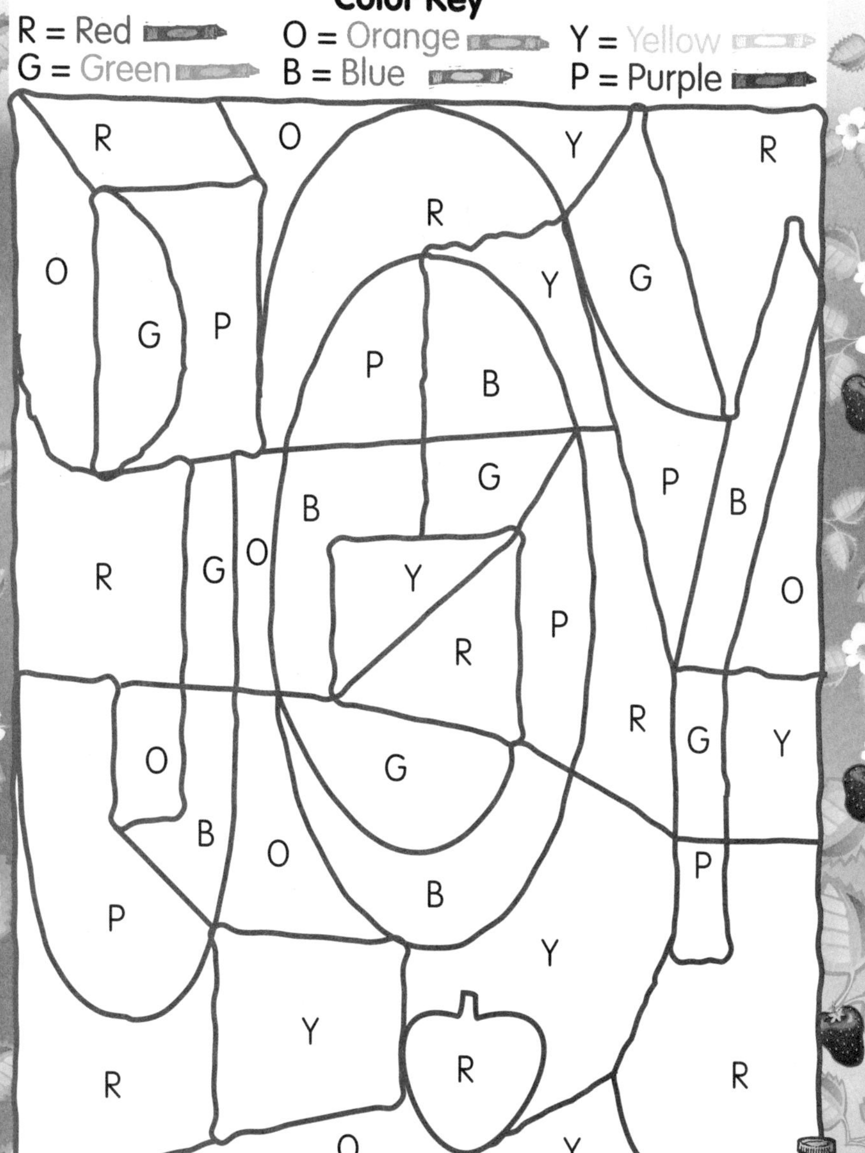

Joyfully Found: One Sheep and a Coin

Luke 15:1-10

The  felt JOY because h

The  was full of JOY becaus

God  s us very much and He

The sheep and coin are lost! Find and circle them.

How many "JOY"s can you find? _______

How many hearts can you find? _______

ɔund the lost [sheep] .

ıe found her lost [coin] .

ll of JOY when we [heart] Him.

Sprout for Joy!
Dear God,
Thank You for
In Jesus' name, amen.

In the spaces below, write words or draw pictures to thank God.

makes me feel joyful.

BIBLE MEMORY VERSE

"The Lord has done great things for us, and we are filled with joy." Psalm 126:3

Some kids enter their rabbits in county fairs. They take good care of their rabbits. They clip the rabbits' nails and brush the rabbits' fur.

Can I have my fur brushed, too?

Uncle Zeke's Corny Tongue Twister

Can you say this three times fast?

Please pass three sweet peas and a piece of peach pie!

Birds' Words

Use the code below to complete the sentence.

When I know God is taking care of me, I have

____ ____ ____ ____ ____ .

Code:

a

c

e

p

Don't Worry—Have Peace

Matthew 4:23-25; 6:25-34; 7:28-29

What did Jesus say about worrying?

- **Start at the red letter G.**
- **Go clockwise around the picture, skipping a letter each time.**

v

d

i

e

g

Do not worry. ______

what you ______

- Write the letters you land on in the blanks below. Go around twice until every letter is used.
- Can you find eight things in the picture that don't belong?

G

e

o

n

d

e

vill ____ ____ ____ ____ you

Worrywarts

These pictures show things that kids sometimes worry about. **Choose a picture and act it out.**

I wasn't invited...

SCHOOL

Why might you worry in these situations?

BIBLE MEMORY VERSE

"My peace I give you. . . . Do not let your hearts be troubled and do not be afraid." John 14:27

What could you do to stop worrying and have peace?

SESSION FOUR

PRODUCE
PATIENCE

Feeding all the animals on a farm takes a long time. This hungry calf isn't very patient!

Got milk?

COW FACTS

No two cows have exactly the same pattern of spots.

A cow can give 200,000 glasses of milk in her lifetime.

barn • chicken • cat • cloud • dirt • fence • hay • sky

Country Crossword

Fill in the missing letters to name objects in the picture. The word inside the squares will tell you today's fruit of the Spirit.

		umpkin
b		rn
ca		
ch		cken
tr		e
fe		ce
tra		tor
hors		

pumpkin • tractor

A Father's Patience Pays Off

Luke 15:11-24

Dear Josh,
I asked Dad for my share of the family money.
He said yes! I'm leaving home to have some fun.

To:
Josh

Dear Josh,
I spent all my money.
Now I have to feed pigs for a job!

To:
Josh

Read the postcards that the son sent to his pen pal, Josh.
Draw a picture on each blank postcard to show what happened.

Dear Josh,
I'm having so much fun!
I'm buying new clothes and having parties with my friends.

To:
Josh

Dear Josh,
I finally came home.
Dad forgave me and took me back as his son!

To:
Josh

Patience, Please!

Read the comics. If someone in the picture is showing patience, draw a smile on the cow. If no one is showing patience, draw a frown on the cow.

Draw a situation where you need to have patience.

BIBLE MEMORY VERSE

"Be completely humble and gentle; be patient."
Ephesians 4:2

Your little sister walks too slow!
FAIR TICKETS
Let's get a wagon, so she can ride with us!
WAGON RENTALS

Draw yourself being patient.

SESSION FIVE

PICK
KINDNESS

These kids show kindness with their prize-winning sheep!

So far the Sheep "R" Us 4-H Club of Lake County, Ohio, has raised three sheep. They sold them and gave the money to a homeless shelter, the Cancer Society and the Ronald McDonald House.

What a "wooly" cool idea!

THE FARM REPORT

Some men from Iowa use their tractors to square dance at county fairs.

Amazing Corn Maze

Be kind and help the lost boy find the way out of the corn maze.

Exit

An Unlikely Hero— The Kind Samaritan

Luke 10:25-37

Number each picture to put the story in the right order. Read the words from each picture in order. What do the words say?

to each other
try to

nd

lways

and to

everyone else.
ROCKY ROAD INN

The Kindness Awards

Cut out the Kindness Awards.
Glue a Kindness Award next to each person you see being kind.
Draw a picture of yourself being kind to someone in the picture.

BIBLE MEMORY VERSE

"Always try to be kind to each other and to everyone else." 1 Thessalonians 5:15

Sticker
Page